Dear Polly,

Gods many blessings to you. So good to see you today.

Love you,

Brenda Sue Randolph

NUGGETS OF TRUTH TO LIVE BY

Brenda Sue Randolph

Trilogy Christian Publishers A Wholly Owned Subsidiary of Trinity Broadcasting Network

2442 Michelle Drive Tustin, CA 92780

Copyright © 2021 by Brenda Sue Randolph

All scripture quotations are taken from the New American Standard Bible. Public domain.

No part of this book may be reproduced, stored in a retrieval system, or transmitted by any means without written permission from the author. All rights reserved. Printed in the USA.

Rights Department, 2442 Michelle Drive, Tustin, CA 92780.

Trilogy Christian Publishing/TBN and colophon are trademarks of Trinity Broadcasting Network.

For information about special discounts for bulk purchases, please contact Trilogy Christian Publishing.

Trilogy Disclaimer: The views and content expressed in this book are those of the author and may not necessarily reflect the views and doctrine of Trilogy Christian Publishing or the Trinity Broadcasting Network.

Manufactured in the United States of America

10 9 8 7 6 5 4 3 2 1

Library of Congress Cataloging-in-Publication Data is available.

ISBN: 978-1-63769-408-4

E-ISBN: 978-1-63769-409-1

ACKNOWLEDGEMENTS

Most importantly, I want to thank God for giving me inspiration for the devotions in this book. Without Him, this book would not have been possible. I have been so blessed to hear His voice clearly in my quiet time with Him. I am so deeply touched that He wants to spend time with me. His desire is to spend time with every person in the world.

I want to especially thank TBN for allowing me to publish this book through them. I am honored to be a partner with you. Mark Mingle was especially helpful in answering all of my questions and explaining the process. Thank you for your kindness. I appreciate you.

A special thank you to my friends and family who encouraged me to continue writing. Thank you to my dad, Jack Mason, who has encouraged me to believe that God would use me to get His word out.

I especially want to thank my dedicated prayer partners Liz Hammond, Sharon Wilson, Herman and Katie Stewart, Julie Graham, Betty Komyatte, Judy Sitko, Gretchen Buchannon, Cindy Taskey, and Georgetta Gilmore for fervently praying for this devotional to be completed.

A very special thank you to my dear granddaughter, Savannah Kiefer, for helping me with all of the technical computer issues and helping with organizing my manuscript. Your help was extremely invaluable to me.

Last, but not least, a special thank you to my husband, Ray, who encouraged me and was completely supportive in my endeavors to write this devotional. I am truly blessed.

Cover photo taken by Mary Jane Cole in Elkview, WV

DEVOTIONAL CONTENTS

Nuggets of Truth to Live By i
Brenda Sue Randolph i
Acknowledgements iii
Introduction 1
A Complete Love 2
A Far-Reaching Love 3
A New Creation 4
A Precious Gift 5
A Pure Heart 6
Abandon Revenge 7
Align Your Thoughts 8
Alive in Christ 9
Angels Around You 10
Anxious Thoughts 11
Authority in Heaven and Earth 12
Available Help 13
Be a Doer of the Word 14
Be an Overcomer 15
Be Content and Satisfied 16
Be Faithful to Me 17
Be Filled 18
Be of Good Cheer 19
Be Thankful 20

Bless Others	21
Blessings are Coming	22
Bonded Together in Love	23
Choose My Plan	24
Circumstances in Life	25
Desire of Your Heart	26
Encouraging Words	27
Focus on Me	28
Focus Your Thoughts	29
Fulfilling My Plan	30
Give in Secret	31
Habits in Life	32
Have No Other gods Before Me	33
He is Faithful	34
Help Your Neighbor	35
Helper and Teacher	36
Hide My Word in Your Heart	37
Humble Yourselves	38
I am Jesus	39
I Deliver My Saints	40
I Give You Power and Strength	41
I Make Intercessions for You	42
I See Through the Dark	43
I Will Deliver You	44
I Will Fight for You	45
Inward Joy	46

Keep Me First	47
Know My Ways	48
Knowledge	49
Light Dawns in Darkness	50
Listen and Obey	51
Live a Life of Love	52
Looking from Heaven	53
Love Comes from My Father	54
Love One Another	55
Love Sincerely	56
Making Decisions	57
Meditate on My Word	58
Meeting Every Need	59
Motives of the Heart	60
Moving Your Mountains	61
My Divine Light	62
My Eyes See All	63
My Father's Glory	64
My Gifts and Calling	65
My Good Plans	66
My Love and Light	67
My Promises are True	68
My Word	69
Not by Your Works	70
Nothing is Hidden	71
Nurture Your Relationship	72

Obedience Brings Blessings 73
Obstacles in Your Path 74
Omnipotent God 75
One True Shepherd 76
Patience Through Trials 77
Peace is a Beautiful Gift 78
Please Me 79
Prayer 80
Pride Versus Humility 81
Reflect My Love 82
Rely on My Strength 83
Renewed in Your Spirit 84
Rivers of Living Water 85
Ruler Over Mankind 86
Sealed with the Holy Spirit 87
Search for Wisdom 88
Searching for Happiness 89
See and Hear Truth 90
Serve Me with Your Whole Heart 91
Shedding of My Blood 92
Sing Songs of Praise 93
Speak Truth 94
Stay Closely Connected to Me 95
Stay Plugged into Me 96
Step into My Thought Pattern 97
Surrender Your Will 98

Take Every Thought Captive	99
Talents Given	100
The Beauty of My Word	101
The Bread of Life	102
The Instruction Manual	103
The Power of My Spirit	104
The Power of Words	105
The Righteousness of God	106
The Ultimate Inheritance	107
The Will of My Father	108
Things Seen are Temporary	109
Thinking Patterns	110
Traditions of Men	111
Transgressions Removed	112
Treasures in My Word	113
Troubled Thoughts	114
True Wisdom	115
Unlock True Joy	116
Wait on Me	117
Walk Uprightly	118
We Are One	119
Wisdom and Understanding	120
Words Heal or Wound	121
Worship Me in Song	122
Your Faith	123
Your Hairs are Numbered	124

Your Heart Speaks 125
Your Steps are Ordered 126
About The Author 127

INTRODUCTION

This devotional was written to help individuals grow spiritually, as they walk alongside the Lord. The principles in this book help remind you that you are not alone in this journey called life. You have all of the help you need, if you but ask. You can enjoy the peace that surpasses all understanding when you keep your focus on Jesus, the author and finisher of your faith. Be thankful for your inward joy when there is chaos all around you.

The truths in this book will open your eyes and help you to see how to live a satisfied life. Spending time in the Word of God is key to experiencing a joy-filled life. You search for happiness in places that do not satisfy. When you choose to stay in the center of God's will, you will be satisfied and have peace and joy as a benefit.

You were saved to serve, and not to sit on the sidelines. God has a purpose and a plan for each of your lives. Experience all that the Lord has waiting for you, by seeking to live out His plan for you. It will bring your joy to overflowing. Don't fear that He will ask you to do tasks above your ability, for He will give you the talents and ability to perform them. Don't be afraid to step out in faith and trust the Lord to accomplish His will through you. You will be amazed by the things you can accomplish with God leading the way.

My prayer would be that you would be transformed as you follow Jesus and His principles for a fulfilling life.

A COMPLETE LOVE

---◆---

When you see Me face to face, then you will have all knowledge. You will be able to know truth. You will see clearly the reasons for obstacles that were in your path. You will know and feel a complete love that overshadows any hurt you may have experienced. My love will engulf your being to the full. My love binds us together in unity. My love is an everlasting love which endures forever. My love never changes, it is the same yesterday, today, and forever.

> For now we see in a mirror dimly, but then face to face; now I know in part, but then I will know fully, just as I also have been fully known.
>
> I Corinthians 13:12

> In addition to all these things *put on* love, which is the perfect bond of unity.
>
> Colossians 3:14

A FAR-REACHING LOVE

I hear your unspoken words within your heart. You're longing to be loved with a pure, undefiled love. Breathe in the deep penetrating love I have waiting for you. Love is such a powerful force in the world. The tentacles of love are far-reaching in every direction. My love for you surpasses all knowledge. It is not easily understood, but undeniable to those who receive it. My love is the greatest gift ever given. Accept the gift of My love and be filled to the measure of all the fullness of God.

> Beloved, let's love one another; for love is from God, and everyone who loves has been born of God and knows God.
>
> I John 4:7

> And to know the love of Christ which surpasses knowledge, that you may be filled to all the fullness of God.
>
> Ephesians 3:19

A NEW CREATION

———◆———

Your relationship with Me affects every aspect of your life. If anyone is in Me, he is a new creation. Old things have passed away and all things have become new. Now you become workers together with Me, as ministers of God. You are the temple of the living God. My Holy Spirit dwells in you. This anointing of the Holy Spirit will teach you concerning all things. This illuminating of power in you will help you to understand what is true or false. His power will light the way before you and give you clear understanding of which avenue to take. Embrace this new life to the full.

> Do you not know that you are a temple of God and *that* the Spirit of God dwells in you?
>
> I Corinthians 3:16

> Now we have not received the spirit of the world, but the Spirit who is from God, so that we may know the things freely given to us by God.
>
> I Corinthians 2:12

A PRECIOUS GIFT

For no one knows the things of God except the Spirit of God. The Spirit reveals truths to you when He lives inside of those who have accepted Me as Lord and Savior. The Holy Spirit imparts truth and wisdom to the believer. The Holy Spirit is such a precious gift to you. It would be impossible to walk in My ways without Him. He intercedes for you when you are broken in spirit, and do not know how to pray. The Holy Spirit will enlighten you to live a life worthy of your calling. Walk in humility, patience, meekness, and love toward your fellow man.

> For who among people knows the *thoughts* of a person except the spirit of the person that is in him? So also the *thoughts* of God no one knows except the Spirit of God.
>
> I Corinthians 2:11

> Now in the same way the Spirit helps our weakness; for we do not know what to pray for as we should, but the Spirt Himself intercedes for *us* with groanings too deep for words.
>
> Romans 8:26

A PURE HEART

Do not give grudgingly due to being greedy. Give cheerfully out of a pure heart. The one who sows sparingly will also reap sparingly, and the one who sows generously will also reap generously. There is true joy in giving to others out of a pure heart. Out of the abundance of one's heart the mouth speaks. When your heart is good, that good will flow out of you. When your heart is evil, that evil will flow out of you. Those who love with a pure heart will love their enemies and do good to those who hate them. They will pray for their enemies. They will give to those in need. They will treat people in the same way that they want to be treated. Seek to have a pure heart.

> Now I *say* this: the one who sows sparingly will also reap sparingly, and the one who sows generously will also reap generously.
>
> 2 Corinthians 9:6

> The good person out of the good treasure of his heart brings forth what is good; and the evil *person* out of the evil *treasure* brings forth what is evil; for his mouth speaks from that which fills *his* heart.
>
> Luke 6:45

ABANDON REVENGE

———◆———

Abandon any thoughts of revenge or anger. This kind of thinking will only cause you harm. Release to Me any thoughts of anger and trust Me to work good out of this situation. Situations will arise that cause issues of anger to rise up in you. Do not hold onto these thoughts, but transfer them to Me. Vengeance is mine, and I will repay them for any evil done to you. All things will occur in My timing. You need to continue walking in love and let Me deal with issues that cause you harm. Let go of anger and watch Me work.

> Cease from anger and abandon wrath; Do not get upset; *it leads* only to evildoing.
>
> Psalms 37:8

> Never take your own revenge, beloved, but leave room for the wrath *of God*, for it is written: "Vengeance is Mine, I will repay," says the Lord.
>
> Romans 12:19

ALIGN YOUR THOUGHTS

———◆———

When you commit all that you do to Me, your thoughts will be aligned with Me. What you are thinking will influence the path you will take for the day. This commitment will keep you on the straight and narrow path that leads to everlasting life. Ponder the path of your feet, and let all your ways be established. Pay attention to My word and listen to what I am telling you. Keep Me in the center of all of your decision-making. I will guide you with My eye upon you. Trust Me to keep you in perfect peace when I am at the forefront of your thoughts.

> Commit your works to the LORD, And your plans will be established.
>
> Proverbs 16:3

> Watch the path of your feet, And all your ways will be established.
>
> Proverbs 4:26

ALIVE IN CHRIST

―――◆―――

When you believe in Me, out of your heart will flow rivers of living water. When you are alive in Me, your life will show others who I am. I will not be hidden from others when my love is flowing from you to them. Streams of water are powerful when they flow quickly downstream. The power of the flow cannot be held back, as with my free-flowing love toward those around you. Let my living water splash onto those who cross your path. The power of my love will be flowing freely onto them.

> The one who believes in Me, as the Scripture said, "From his innermost being will flow rivers of living water."
>
> John 7:38

> For as in Adam all die, so also in Christ all will be made alive.
>
> I Corinthians 15:22

ANGELS AROUND YOU

———◆———

My angels are watching over you, to keep you safe and protected. They are near and around you at all times, although mostly unseen. There are times I reveal an angel's presence to you, for my purpose of growth for you. Do not forget to entertain strangers, for one could be an angel sent by Me to grow your faith. The angels joyfully worship Me and obey My word. I have sent angels ahead of you to guard you along your way. You can rest easy knowing you are protected.

> For it is written: 'HE WILL GIVE HIS ANGELS ORDERS CONCERNING YOU, TO PROTECT YOU.'
>
> Luke 4:10

> Do not neglect hospitality to strangers, for by this some have entertained angels without knowing it.
>
> Hebrews 13:2

ANXIOUS THOUGHTS

Do not be anxious, thinking, *how will I solve this problem?* Bring your problems and cares to Me and lay them at my feet. I am fully capable of taking care of them. Ask for my wisdom on how to respond to this problem. Put your hope in Me and your strength will be renewed. You will be able to run and not grow weary. You will have the power to move forward without fear. Remember there is nothing too difficult for Me. You can enjoy peace and rest when you trust Me to handle your problems. Many are the afflictions of the righteous, but I will deliver you out of them all.

> Yet those who wait for the LORD will gain new strength; they will mount up *with* wings like eagles, they will run and not get tired, they will walk and not become weary.
>
> Isaiah 40:31

> The afflictions of the righteous are many, But the LORD rescues him from them all.
>
> Psalms 34:19

AUTHORITY IN HEAVEN AND EARTH

My Father has given Me all authority in heaven and on earth. You who know Me personally are complete in Me, who is the head over every ruler in authority. Being complete in Me gives you more than enough to sustain you through this life. Being complete in Me allows you to hand over the control of your life to Me. I will direct and guide you through your life's journey. I will give you the tools to help you have victory in all circumstances you face. There are those who have some authority on earth, but remember, I have been given *all* authority in heaven and on earth.

> And Jesus came up and spoke to them, saying, "All authority in heaven and on earth has been given to Me."
>
> Matthew 28:18

> And in Him you have been made complete, and He is the head over every ruler and authority.
>
> Colossians 2:10

AVAILABLE HELP

I will set a guard over your mouth and keep watch over the door of your lips when you ask Me to. I am always available to help you with your needs. I am waiting to hear your precious voice call out to Me. We are partners in this life, from the time you asked me into your heart. My heart leapt with joy when you invited Me into your life. I take our relationship seriously. Give Me the opportunity to help you with your daily tasks. I do not override your will, but wait patiently for you to seek My will in your life decisions. Your journey through life will be blessed when you let go of the reins and let Me guide you.

> Set a guard, LORD, over my mouth; keep watch over the door of my lips.
>
> Psalms 141:3

> I can do nothing on My own. As I hear, I judge; and My judgment is righteous, because I do not seek My own will but the will of Him who sent Me.
>
> John 5:30

BE A DOER OF THE WORD

If you are a hearer of the Word, and do not implement these truths into action, you will lose the blessings you could have received. Your actions reveal your level of commitment to Me. Open your heart to hear what I am teaching you in My Word. Read My Word to receive instruction for how to live your life each day. Know that I will give you the power to live out My instruction given to you. Do not let fear stop your obedience, because I will give you the strength to accomplish all things through Me.

> But one who has looked intently at the perfect law, the *law* of freedom, and has continued *in it*, not having become a forgetful hearer but an active doer, this person will be blessed in what he does.
>
> James 1:25

> I can do all things through Him who strengthens me.
>
> Philippians 4:13

BE AN OVERCOMER

I will help you to be an overcomer when you receive Me as Lord and Savior of your life. Those who overcome shall be clothed in white garments and their names shall be written down in the book of life. I will confess their names before My Father and before his angels. When you profess Me in faith, believing and submitting to Me, I will help you overcome the obstacles that you face in life. You will need to abide in My word to know the truth, and the truth shall make you free. Walk close by My side, and partake of the spiritual food of my Word. Man shall not live by bread alone, but by every word that proceeds from the mouth of God.

> The one who overcomes will be clothed the same way, in white garments; and I will not erase his name from the book of life, and I will confess his name before My Father and before His angels.
>
> Revelation 3:5

> But He answered and said, "It is written: 'MAN SHALL NOT LIVE ON BREAD ALONE, BUT ON EVERY WORD THAT COMES OUT OF THE MOUTH OF GOD.'"
>
> Matthew 4:4

BE CONTENT AND SATISFIED

---◆---

I satisfy your hunger and thirst for life. I am the bread of life. The one who comes to Me will not be hungry, and the one who believes in Me will never be thirsty. No one can come to Me unless the Father who sent Me draws him; and I will raise him up on the last day. You will be content when you allow Me to transform the way you think. Many battles are won through the transformation of your thoughts. My dear friends keep your minds on whatever is true, pure, right, holy, friendly, and proper. Don't ever stop thinking about what is truly worthwhile and worthy of praise.

> Jesus said to them, "I am the bread of life; the one who comes to Me will not be hungry, and the one who believes in Me will never be thirsty.
>
> John 6:35
>
> No one can come to Me unless the Father who sent Me draws him; and I will raise him up on the last day.
>
> John 6:44

BE FAITHFUL TO ME

When you are faithful to Me, I will instruct My angels to watch over you and guard you. My angels are ministering spirits sent forth to minister to those who will inherit salvation. Rejoice in the fact that I have made provision to care for My own. Cast all your anxiety on Me because I will take care of you. I will never permit the righteous to be moved. I am forgiving and good, abounding in love to all who call to Me. As the Father has loved Me, so have I loved you. Abide in My love. If you keep My commandments you will abide in My love.

> Are they not all ministering spirits, sent out to *provide* service for the sake of those who will inherit salvation?
>
> Hebrews 1:14

> Just as the Father has loved Me, I also have loved you; remain in My love.
>
> John 15:9

BE FILLED

When you hunger and thirst for righteousness, you will be filled. Come to Me and I will fill you with all that you will ever need. What I give you will satisfy your hungry soul. Listen carefully to Me and eat what is good. Let your soul delight itself in abundance. Whoever drinks of the water that I give him will never thirst. This water will become a fountain of water springing up into everlasting life. The world and its desires pass away, but whoever does the will of My Father lives forever. Come to Me and be filled.

> Why do you spend money for what is not bread, and your wages for what does not satisfy? Listen carefully to Me, and eat what is good, and delight yourself in abundance.
>
> Isaiah 55:2

> The world is passing away and *also* its lusts; but the one who does the will of God continues *to live* forever.
>
> I John 2:17

BE OF GOOD CHEER

No matter what is going on in your life, you can still have peace. It is in Me that you have peace. In the world you will have tribulation, but be of good cheer, for I have overcome the world. The righteous will have many afflictions, but I will deliver you out of them all. Those who hate the righteous will be condemned. None of those who trust in Me will be condemned. I will be a shield for those who love and trust Me. Your reward shall be very great. Enjoy My peace and trust Me for the deliverance of your afflictions.

> These things I have spoken to you so that in Me you may have peace. In the world you have tribulation, but take courage; I have overcome the world.
>
> John 16:33
>
> The afflictions of the righteous are many, but the LORD rescues him from them all.
>
> Psalms 34:19

BE THANKFUL

---◆---

Be thankful today for all the many blessings I have given you. Be thankful for My love, joy, and peace that surpasses all understanding. My love for you is all encompassing, and beyond your understanding. It reaches out to all humankind with a power that cannot be contained. Remember that I have inscribed you on the palms of My hands. For many waters cannot quench My love for you. When you keep My commandments, you will abide in My love and receive joy to the full. I also give you the gift of peace that the world cannot give you. Receive My gifts today and be ever thankful.

> Behold, I have inscribed you on the palms of *My hands;* your walls are continually before Me.
>
> Isaiah 49:16

> These things I have spoken to you so that My joy may be in you, and *that* your joy may be made full.
>
> John 15:11

BLESS OTHERS

When you serve others, you serve Me. When I give you blessings, use a portion to bless others. You are planting seeds of faith when you bless others around you. When you have a deep love for Me, you will desire to share and give of what I have blessed you with. When you give, let it be from pure motives of your heart. Do not give in a reluctant resentful manner. Give to others out of a cheerful heart, which pleases Me. Give and it will be given back to you in good measure, pressed down, shaken together, and running over into your lap. You cannot out-give Me.

> Each one *must do* just as he has decided in his heart, not reluctantly or under compulsion, for God loves a cheerful giver.
>
> 2 Corinthians 9:7

> Give, and it will be given to you. They will pour into your lap a good measure—pressed down, shaken together, *and* running over. For by your standard of measure it will be measured to you in return.
>
> Luke 6:38

BLESSINGS ARE COMING

No eye has seen, or ear heard what blessings are coming to those who love Me with all of their heart. The mind cannot comprehend the beauty of what is to come to those who know Me personally. My precious children will live in the light of My love forever. Your body will be transformed into the likeness of My glorious body. I go to prepare a place for you, that where I am you may be also. My promises are true and will come to pass in My perfect timing. Await earnestly for your blessings are coming.

> But just as it is written: "THINGS WHICH EYE HAS NOT SEEN AND EAR HAS NOT HEARD, AND WHICH HAVE NOT ENTERED THE HUMAN HEART, ALL THAT GOD HAS PREPARED FOR THOSE WHO LOVE HIM."
>
> I Corinthians 2:9
>
> And if I go and prepare a place for you, I am coming again and will take you to Myself, so that where I am, *there* you also will be.
>
> John 14:3

BONDED TOGETHER IN LOVE

———◆———

When you are bonded to something or someone, you are securely joined together. My love bonds us together securely. When you spend substantial time with Me, we are bonded together. Together the power of My love will transform the attitudes of those around you. Love binds everything together in perfect harmony. When we live in harmony, our lives are flowing peacefully with one another. Join Me in living a life of love to those around you. The power of My love will cast out any fear or doubt from your mind. Perfect love casts out any fear in your life. Stay securely bonded to Me through the power of My love.

> In addition to all these things *put on* love, which is the perfect bond of unity.
>
> Colossians 3:14

> There is no fear in love, but perfect love drives out fear, because fear involves punishment, and the one who fears is not perfected in love.
>
> I John 4:18

CHOOSE MY PLAN

―――◆―――

Living close to Me will keep you from thinking there is no harm in doing this one time. Anything that makes you say this action will not harm me one time, is wrong. Living close to Me will set off a loud alarm to any thinking like this. Rebuke the devil and he will flee from you. Commit to living a life of obedience to Me, and you will escape the pitfalls the devil has planned for you. His plan is to steal, kill, and destroy. My plan is to give you an abundant and satisfying life. Common sense and wisdom would say, choose my plan and have an abundant, satisfying life.

> Submit therefore to God. But resist the devil, and he will flee from you.
>
> James 4:7

> The thief comes only to steal and kill and destroy; I came so that they would have life, and have *it* abundantly.
>
> John 10:10

CIRCUMSTANCES IN LIFE

Your circumstances in life are not what bring peace and a feeling of security to you. You will go through different circumstances, good times, and bad times, but you can experience peace through it all. Your thoughts are resting securely in Me when I am at the forefront of your mind. When you seek Me first and My righteousness, all of your needs will be met. You can be secure in knowing that I am working all things for your good, for those who love Me and are called according to My purpose. Do not let your circumstances influence how you serve Me. Use every circumstance as an opportunity to be a light in this dark world.

> But seek first His kingdom and His righteousness, and all these things will be provided to you.
>
> Matthew 6:33

> And we know that God causes all things to work together for good to those who love God, to those who are called according to *His* purpose.
>
> Romans 8:28

DESIRE OF YOUR HEART

When I am the desire of your heart, you will be satisfied. Hope deferred makes the heart sick, but desire fulfilled is a tree of life. A desire accomplished is sweet to the soul. Desire to transform your mind so you will know My Father's will for you. My Father's will is good, acceptable, and perfect. Owe nothing to anyone except to love one another. Treat people the same way you want them to treat you. If possible, so far as it depends on you, be at peace with all people. My Father's will is that you love Him with all your heart, and that you love your neighbor as yourself.

> Hope deferred makes the heart sick, but desire fulfilled is a tree of life.
>
> Proverbs 13:12

> And do not be conformed to this world, but be transformed by the renewing of your mind, so that you may prove what the will of God is, that which is good and acceptable and perfect.
>
> Romans 12:2

ENCOURAGING WORDS

Pleasant words spoken are like a honeycomb, sweet to the soul and healing to the bones. Words spoken are so powerful. They can bring healing to the body. Pleasant words are pure in My sight. Use encouraging words to those around you to build them up in the faith. Pleasant words show My love flowing through you to others. A gentle answer turns away wrath, but a harsh word stirs up anger. It is wise to be able to control your tongue and keep My spirit of love flowing through you.

> Pleasant words are a honeycomb, sweet to the soul and healing to the bones.
>
> Proverbs 16:24

> A gentle answer turns away wrath, but a harsh word stirs up anger.
>
> Proverbs 15:1

FOCUS ON ME

Focus on Me and your life will flow more easily throughout the day. Choose to focus your thoughts on Me and the challenges of the day will not overtake you. I will enfold you in my arms and give you peace and rest in your spirit. The troubles of the day will seem insignificant when your focus is on Me. I will guard your heart and your mind so that you can live in perfect peace. I am the gift that keeps on giving. Focus on Me, the ultimate gift-giver, and enjoy My peace and rest.

> The steadfast of mind You will keep in perfect peace, because he trusts in You.
>
> Isaiah 26:3

> And the peace of God, which surpasses all comprehension, will guard your hearts and minds in Christ Jesus.
>
> Philippians 4:7

FOCUS YOUR THOUGHTS

———◆———

There is nothing hidden from Me, for I know your thoughts. I am acquainted with all your ways. Let Me mold and make you after My will, that you will have innumerable blessings in life. When you let Me transform your thoughts, you will live a life that is pleasing to Me. Do not be distracted by the evil going on around you, but keep your thoughts and mind focused on what I am doing. I have given each person different gifts to be used for the building up of the whole body. Continue using your gifts so that others will be encouraged, and harmony will flourish among My people.

> You scrutinize my path and my lying down, and are acquainted with all my ways.
>
> Psalms 139:3

> And do not be conformed to this world, but be transformed by the renewing of your mind, so that you may prove what the will of God is, that which is good and acceptable and perfect.
>
> Romans 12:2

FULFILLING MY PLAN

My father will honor anyone who serves Me. I came, not to be served, but to serve and give My life as a ransom for many. My desire would be for you to look out for the needs of those around you. When I show you a need, then you are the one to fulfill that need. Serve and love others with a joyful spirit, so I will be reflected through you. Let your light shine before others that they may see your good deeds and glorify your Father in heaven. When you serve others, you are serving Me, and fulfilling My plan for you.

> If anyone serves Me, he must follow Me; and where I am, there My servant will be also; if anyone serves Me, the Father will honor him.
>
> John 12:26

> Your light must shine before people in such a way that they may see your good works, and glorify your Father who is in heaven.
>
> Matthew 5:16

GIVE IN SECRET

Do not practice your righteousness for others to see your goodness. There is great temptation to want others to know the good you are doing. You love the praise of men. So much better would be the reward of My Father in heaven. When your charitable giving is done in secret, My Father will reward you openly. I am always looking at the motives of your heart. Stay close to Me so your motives will be pure. Your goal should be to love from a pure heart, from a good conscience, and from a sincere faith. Walk in step with Me throughout the day and receive your rewards.

> Take care not to practice your righteousness in the sight of people, to be noticed by them; otherwise you have no reward with your Father who is in heaven.
> Matthew 6:1

> But the goal of our instruction is love from a pure heart, *from* a good conscience, and *from* a sincere faith.
> I Timothy 1:5

HABITS IN LIFE

When you repeat something in your daily life, it becomes a habit to do so. You can have good habits or bad habits. When you come to Me throughout the day and read My Word, it becomes part of your daily habit. It is part of your normal routine. Therefore, be imitators of My Father as beloved children, and walk in love. Get in the habit of following the teachings of My Word. Forgive quickly when you are offended. Be kind to one another, tenderhearted, forgiving each other, just as My Father has forgiven you. Follow My teachings, and stay away from creating bad habits that cause you to stumble.

> Therefore be imitators of God, as beloved children; and walk in love, just as Christ also loved you and gave Himself up for us, an offering and a sacrifice to God as a fragrant aroma.
>
> Ephesians 5:1-2

> Be kind to one another, compassionate, forgiving each other, just as God in Christ also has forgiven you.
>
> Ephesians 4:32

HAVE NO OTHER GODS BEFORE ME

―――◆―――

Be careful that you put no other gods before Me. For I am a jealous God. It is easy to get into the mindset of putting things before Me. What you spend the most time thinking about or engaging in may be a problem. Make sure you are consulting Me about the activities of your days. Whether you turn to the right or to the left, your ears will hear a voice behind you saying, "This is the way, walk in it." Continually seek Me for direction. I will satisfy all of your needs and guide you along the path of life.

> You shall have no other gods before Me.
>
> Exodus 20:3

> Your ears will hear a word behind you, saying, "This is the way, walk in it," whenever you turn to the right or to the left.
>
> Isaiah 30:21

HE IS FAITHFUL

―――◆―――

Do you hear My call to you? Are you listening to My still small voice? He who calls you is faithful, who will also do it. I will establish you and guard you from the evil one. Do not let your faith be in the wisdom of men, but in the power of God. Oh, the deep richness of the wisdom and knowledge of God! How unsearchable are His judgments and unfathomable His ways! For from Him and through Him and to Him are all things. You will do well to heed the prophetic word as a light that shines in a dark place, until the day dawns and the morning star rises in your hearts. Listen to my still small voice.

> But the Lord is faithful, and He will strengthen and protect you from the evil one.
>
> 2 Thessalonians 3:3

> Oh, the depth of the riches, both of the wisdom and knowledge of God! How unsearchable are His judgments and unfathomable His ways!
>
> Romans 11:33

HELP YOUR NEIGHBOR

When you encounter a neighbor in need, and you have the power to help them, do so. Do not say to them go and come back tomorrow and I will help you. This would be a missed opportunity to be My hands and feet. Listen to My voice and be a blessing, and in turn you will be blessed. This power to help shows My love in action. One is wise who listens and follows My leading in their life. These opportunities of supplying one's needs in love will bring joy unspeakable into your life. There is great joy in giving to others and being a light to them in dark days. Do not miss any opportunities that I lay before you. Be a blessing and you will be blessed.

> Do not say to your neighbor, "Go and come back, and tomorrow I will give *it to you,*" when you have it with you.
>
> Proverbs 3:28

> And do not neglect doing good and sharing, for with such sacrifices God is pleased.
>
> Hebrews 13:16

HELPER AND TEACHER

My Holy Spirit will bring to your mind things that are needful to live a life dedicated to Me. He is your Helper and your teacher. Be attentive to listen and learn from my Holy Spirit. This will help you be successful in accomplishing My will for you. Peace and joy in life will be a benefit of listening and learning how to live a life centered on Me and My plan. My plan will be accomplished by your obedience to listen and learn from My guiding Spirit. For if you live according to the flesh you will die, but if you live by the Holy Spirit, and you put to death the deeds of the body, you will live.

> But the Helper, the Holy Spirit whom the Father will send in My name, He will teach you all things, and remind you of all that I said to you.
>
> John 14:26

> For if you are living in accord with the flesh, you are going to die; but if by the Spirit you are putting to death the deeds of the body, you will live.
>
> Romans 8:13

HIDE MY WORD IN YOUR HEART

Hide My Word in your heart that you might not sin against Me. Meditate on My Word and keep it close to your heart. I have given you instructions on how to live a life pleasing to Me. My Word will be a lamp to your feet and a light to your path. You will not have to question in which way you should go. The choices you have to make will be made clear to you. All scripture is God-breathed and useful for teaching, rebuking, correcting, and training in righteousness. This will equip you to follow the path I show you. Saturate your heart and mind in My Word to equip you for success in life.

> I have treasured Your word in my heart, so that I may not sin against you.
>
> Psalms 119:11

> Your word is a lamp to my feet and a light to my path.
>
> Psalms 119:105

HUMBLE YOURSELVES

It is so easy for you to take credit for the things I am doing in your life. Humble yourself before Me and understand the full power of my Holy Spirit working within you. My Holy Spirit is giving you the resources to get My will accomplished. Do not accept the praises of man and be puffed up in your spirit. Without my help, you could not accomplish these tasks given to you. Recognize that I am working in and through you daily. When you humble yourself before me, I will lift you up at the proper time.

> An arrogant person stirs up strife, but one who trusts in the Lord will prosper.
>
> Proverbs 28:25

> Humble yourselves in the presence of the Lord, and He will exalt you.
>
> James 4:10

I AM JESUS

---·◆·---

I am Jesus, the way, the truth, and the life. No one can have access to My Father except through Me. I came down from heaven to do the will of My Father. Accept the sacrifice that I made, by laying down My life for you. This gives you a freedom and a hope for the future. Nourish our relationship by getting to know Me through My Word and conversing with Me. I am interested in every aspect of your life. Share with Me your deepest longings, and your everyday thoughts. Nothing is too trivial to bring to Me, for I am the way, the truth, and the life.

> Jesus said to him, "I am the way, and the truth, and the life; no one comes to the Father except through Me."
>
> John 14:6

> For I have come down from heaven, not to do My own will, but the will of Him who sent Me.
>
> John 6:38

I DELIVER MY SAINTS

You who love Me, hate evil. I preserve the souls of My Saints. I deliver them out of the hand of the wicked. Serve Me with gladness, and come before My presence with singing. I have redeemed your life from destruction and have crowned you with loving-kindness and tender mercies. Give Me thanks for all that I do for you. Make known My deeds among the peoples. Remember the blessings I have given to you throughout your life. Reflecting on these blessings will strengthen you to move forward with Me. For I go with you to fight for you against your enemies, to give you the victory.

> Hate evil, you who love the LORD, who watches over the souls of His godly ones; He saves them from the hand of the wicked.
>
> Psalms 97:10

> For the LORD your God is the One who is going with you, to fight for you against your enemies, to save you.
>
> Deuteronomy 20:4

I GIVE YOU POWER AND STRENGTH

I can give you the power to overcome, and strengthen you in any situation you face. Do not be afraid for I am with you and will strengthen and help you. I will uphold you with My righteous right hand. Focus your thoughts on Me and relax as you watch Me work on your behalf. Trust Me to bring good out of any bad situation. I will preserve you from all evil. I guard the paths of the just and protect the way of My faithful ones. I give power to the weak, and to those who have no might I increase their strength. Wait on Me, and I will give you all the strength you need to overcome.

> Do not fear, for I am with you; do not be afraid, for I am your God. I will strengthen you, I will also help you, I also will uphold you with My righteous right hand.
> Isaiah 41:10

> The LORD will protect you from all evil; He will keep your soul.
> Psalms 121:7

I MAKE INTERCESSIONS FOR YOU

When you are going through hardships, I am at the right hand of My Father making intercessions for you. I stand ready to nurture and care for My sheep. I lovingly guide you along the path of life. I keep watch over you day and night. My ways are higher than your ways and My thoughts higher than your thoughts. Ask Me to guide you, and listen for My voice to give you direction. I want you to involve Me in all aspects of your daily life. It gives Me pleasure to guide you in a way that brings blessings in abundance to your days. I am waiting to hear the sound of your voice seeking My will for you. Ask, and it shall be given to you; seek, and you shall find; knock and it shall be opened to you.

> Who is the one who condemns? Christ Jesus is He who died, but rather, was raised, who is at the right hand of God, who also intercedes for us.
>
> Romans 8:34

> Ask, and it will be given to you; seek, and you will find; knock, and it will be opened to you.
>
> Matthew 7:7

I SEE THROUGH THE DARK

You cannot hide from Me in the dark of the night, for the darkness and the light are both alike to Me. I formed your inward parts and covered you in your mother's womb. You are fearfully and wonderfully made. You are precious in My sight. I have inscribed you on the palms of My hands. My plans are to give you a hope and a future. Trust Me to guide you down the path of life, for I know you completely. There will be bumps along the path, but I will see you safely through your journey. Remember, I can see through the dark of night.

> Even darkness is not dark to You, and the night is as bright as the day. Darkness and light are alike *to You.*
>
> Psalms 139:12

> Behold, I have inscribed you on the palms *of My hands;* your walls are continually before Me.
>
> Isaiah 49:16

I WILL DELIVER YOU

When you set your love upon Me, I will deliver you. I will be with you when trouble comes. I will treasure you and draw near to you. Do not be anxious about anything, but in every situation tell Me what you need and thank Me for all I have done. Keep the doors of communication open with Me. Know that I am working on your behalf even if you do not see the evidence at this time. Put complete trust in Me that I am working things out for your good. For we know that all things work together for good to those who love Me.

> Because he has loved Me, I will save him; I will set him *securely* on high, because he has known My name.
>
> Psalms 91:14

> Do not be anxious about anything, but in everything by prayer and pleading with thanksgiving let your requests be made known to God.
>
> Philippians 4:6

I WILL FIGHT FOR YOU

———◆———

I will fight for you, you need only to be still and watch what I will do. Rest in Me. Give Me your burdens, and I will hold you up. I will not allow you to be shaken. You can trust Me to do what I say. You will be able to overwhelmingly conquer all things through Me, who loves you. I know your needs and the deepest desires of your heart. I will be your strength and your shield. I will fill you with joy and hope as you wait and watch Me conquer your problems for you. The Holy Spirit will give you the power to release your burdens to Me. Continue in prayer and trust Me to fight for you.

> Cast your burden upon the Lord and He will sustain you; He will never allow the righteous to be shaken.
> Psalms 55:22

> But in all these things we overwhelmingly conquer through Him who loved us.
> Romans 8:37

INWARD JOY

Be thankful for the inward joy when circumstances around you are in chaos. You can still have peace on the inside when circumstances do not seem to be going your way. There can continue to be a calm in the midst of your storm. Remember to keep your thoughts focused on Me, knowing I can calm any raging storm. Keep your eyes on Me when the boat appears to be sinking. I will get you safely to shore. Storms in life will come and go but remember if I am steering the boat you will come through the storm safely. Rest in the fact that I am always with you in the good times and in the difficult seasons of your life. The inward joy I give you is your strength.

> Now may the God of hope fill you with all joy and peace in believing, so that you will abound in hope by the power of the Holy Spirit.
>
> Romans 15:13

> He caused the storm to be still, so that the waves of the sea were hushed.
>
> Psalms 107:29

KEEP ME FIRST

When you keep Me first in your life, there is so much that I can accomplish through you. Keep Me a priority in your life, and you will have everything you need. You will receive the help you need to meet the challenges of the day. When the busyness of your activities squeezes Me out of first place, it will be more difficult to deal with challenges that arise. When you abide in Me, you will bear much fruit. Staying connected to the vine will allow you to accomplish My will, for apart from Me, you can do nothing. Abide in Me and give Me first place so you will bear much fruit for the kingdom.

> But seek first His kingdom and His righteousness, and all these things will be provided to you.
>
> Matthew 6:33

> I am the vine, you are the branches; the one who remains in Me, and I in him bears much fruit, for apart from Me you can do nothing.
>
> John 15:5

KNOW MY WAYS

When you read My Word, you will know My ways. If you love Me, you will keep My commandments. Ask Me to reveal My ways to you, for I am the way, the truth, and the life. Life will have fulfillment and meaning when you read My instruction manual. All scripture is inspired by God and profitable for teaching, reproof, correction, and training in righteousness. By this, the man of God may be adequate and equipped for every good work. It is always necessary to read instruction manuals if you want things to fit in their proper place. When you don't read the instructions first, you may have to start over. Start your day in My Word so everything fits in its proper place. Your day will have a better flow to it, with training in righteousness.

> If you love Me, you will keep My commandments.
>
> John 14:15

> All scripture is inspired by God and beneficial for teaching, for rebuke, for correction, for training in righteousness; so that the man *or woman* of God may be fully capable, equipped for every good work.
>
> 2 Timothy 3:16-17

KNOWLEDGE

Clothe yourselves with humility toward one another because My Father is opposed to the proud, but gives grace to the humble. Knowledge can make one conceited, but love edifies people. Do not be proud in the knowledge that you have, but walk humbly with My Father and He will lift you up. For everyone who exalts himself will be humbled, and the one who humbles himself will be exalted. Where does your knowledge come from? For I give wisdom and from My mouth come knowledge and understanding. The mind of the discerning acquires knowledge, and the ear of the wise seeks knowledge.

> You younger men, likewise, be subject to *your* elders; and all of you, clothe yourselves with humility toward one another, because GOD IS OPPOSED TO THE PROUD, BUT HE GIVES GRACE TO THE HUMBLE.
>
> I Peter 5:5
>
> The mind of the discerning acquires knowledge, and the ear of the wise seeks knowledge.
>
> Proverbs 18:15

LIGHT DAWNS IN DARKNESS

———◆———

When you show kindness to those who are hungry or to those who are needy, then your light shall dawn in the darkness. My light will be shining brightly through you for all to see. Any evil deeds done in the dark will come to light. Secrets will be uncovered and known, for all things concealed or hidden will be brought out to the light. Examine these two concepts about My light and what it reveals about man. Choose to let your light shine brightly through kindness, glorifying Me. Do not choose to do evil deeds that will be revealed in time and come to light.

> And *if* you offer yourself to the hungry and satisfy the need of the afflicted, then your light will rise in darkness, and your gloom *will become* like midday.
>
> Isaiah 58:10

> For nothing is concealed that will not become evident, nor *anything* hidden that will not be known and come to light.
>
> Luke 8:17

LISTEN AND OBEY

If you really want to be happy in life, then let Me guide you. I want what will make you happy. If you want blessings to the full, listen and obey My voice. I want what is best for you. When I speak to you about doing something, know that I will give you the power to accomplish it. When you listen and obey My voice, you will see My power manifested through you. This will cause you to grow deeper in your love for Me. Join Me on this journey, and your faith and trust in Me will grow as you listen and obey.

> And the people said to Joshua, "We will serve the Lord our God and obey His voice."
>
> Joshua 24:24

> So faith *comes* from hearing, and hearing by the word of Christ.
>
> Romans 10:17

LIVE A LIFE OF LOVE

It would please Me to see you live a life of love. What does love look like? Love is patient and kind. Love does not insist on its own way, but is more concerned about the needs of others. Love does not envy or boast. Love is not concerned about what others around you possess. Love has the characteristics of humility and kindness to all people. Love is a uniting force in the world. Ask Me to make your love increase and overflow for everyone you meet. In doing so, it will draw them to Me, for love is from God.

> Love is patient, love is kind, it is not jealous; love does not brag, it is not arrogant.
>
> I Corinthians 13:4

> Beloved, let's love one another; for love is from God, and everyone who loves has been born of God and knows God.
>
> I John 4:7

LOOKING FROM HEAVEN

I look from heaven and see all the sons of mankind. From My dwelling place, I look out on all the inhabitants of the earth. What will I see you doing? Are you caught up in the busyness of life? All things are permitted, but not all things are of benefit. All things are permitted, but not all things build people up. Choose wisely how you spend your time, and for what it profits. Do not forget that I want to be involved in all of your decision-making throughout the day. I make firm the steps of the one who delights in Me; though he may stumble, he will not fall, for I uphold him with My hand.

> The Lord looks from heaven; He sees all the sons of mankind; from His dwelling place He looks out, on all the inhabitants of the earth.
> Psalms 33:13-14

> All things are permitted, but not all things are of benefit. All things are permitted, but not all things build *people* up.
> I Corinthians 10:23

LOVE COMES FROM MY FATHER

When you show love to all of mankind, this pleases Me. Love is a very powerful gift. Love binds everything together in perfect harmony. Love is patient and kind and does not envy or boast. It is not arrogant or rude. Love does not insist on its own way. When you are full of love for others, they are drawn to this power in you. Harmony and peace will flow when love is present. Love comes from My Father, and whoever loves has been born of Him and knows Him. Let all that you do be done in love.

> In addition to all these things *put on* love, which is the perfect bond of unity.
>
> Colossians 3:14

> For now we see in a mirror dimly, but then face to face; now I know in part, but then I will know fully, just as I also have been fully known.
>
> I Corinthians 13:12

LOVE ONE ANOTHER

When you keep My commandments, it shows Me you are abiding in My love. Keeping My Father's commandments shows I am abiding in His love. Let us remain in this love that never fails. Love is the greatest command that is given. Everyone who truly loves is born of God and knows Him. Love is shown by your actions toward others. When this powerful love shines through you to others, this will draw them to Me. Love is overpowering in its pull to draw people to it. Keep my commandment to love one another.

> Beloved, let's love one another; for love is from God, and everyone who loves has been born of God and knows God.
>
> I John 4:7

> I am giving you a new commandment, that you love one another; just as I have loved you, that you also love one another.
>
> John 13:34

LOVE SINCERELY

———◆———

Do not be a hypocrite when loving others. Be genuine in your love for others. Detest what is evil and cling to what is good. Be devoted to one another in brotherly love. Honor and choose to fulfill other's needs before your own. Love must be sincere. When I reveal a need someone has, then I would like you to be the one to take care of it. Do not ask Me to take care of other's needs when you have the ability to do so. Step forward and show your sincere love for those in need. Do what is right in the sight of all people. Never repay evil for evil to anyone. Do not be overcome by evil, but overcome evil with good. Love sincerely.

> Love *must be* free of hypocrisy. Detest what is evil; cling to what is good.
>
> Romans 12:9

> Never repay evil for evil to anyone. Respect what is right in the sight of all people.
>
> Romans 12:17

MAKING DECISIONS

I should be in the center of your thoughts as you make decisions in your life. Let pleasing Me be the passion of your heart. Do you know that your body is a temple where the Holy Spirit resides? Be thankful for this awesome power within you and glorify God in your body. Listen as the Holy Spirit reveals wisdom to you, about decisions you need to make. God will be glorified through you, as you listen and follow down the path He shows you. This will increase your faith. Even faith as tiny as a mustard seed can accomplish seemingly impossible tasks.

> Or do you not know that your body is a temple of the Holy Spirit within you, whom you have from God, and *that* you are not your own?
>
> I Corinthians 6:19

> And He said to them, "Because of your meager faith; for truly I say to you, if you have faith the size of a mustard seed, you will say to this mountain, 'Move from here to there,' and it will move; and nothing will be impossible for you."
>
> Matthew 17:20

MEDITATE ON MY WORD

———◆———

When you meditate on My Word day and night, you shall have a prosperous successful life. You will be reaping wisdom on how to please Me. You will enjoy My blessings and favor when you desire to seek My will for you. Keep My words flowing through your thoughts, that you may be encouraged to make wise decisions. My guidance will keep you on the straight and narrow path to joy and peace. Let your heart retain My words of wisdom and receive My instruction. The fear of the Lord is the beginning of wisdom. I will keep in perfect peace those whose minds are steadfast because they trust in me.

> But his delight is in the Law of the LORD, and on His Law he meditates day and night.
>
> Psalms 1:2

> The steadfast of mind You will keep in perfect peace, because he trusts in You.
>
> Isaiah 26:3

MEETING EVERY NEED

———◆———

My promises are true, and I do not abandon any who seek Me. I will meet your every need. When your trial overwhelms you, do not be afraid, just keep trusting Me. I am strong enough to carry any burden that weighs you down. Cast that burden on Me and I will sustain you. You can trust Me with your life. With Me by your side, nothing will be impossible for you. Do not be afraid of what man can do to you, but stand firm, and you will see My deliverance. For I am ready to meet your every need.

> And those who know Your name will put their trust in You, For You, Lord, have not abandoned those who seek You.
>
> Psalms 9:10
>
> For nothing will be impossible with God.
>
> Luke 1:37

MOTIVES OF THE HEART

As My follower, I would desire that your actions and motives would be pure. My desire would be that what you are doing in My name, would be done with a pure heart. Your motives should not be about receiving praise from men, but about praising your Father in heaven. Examine your motives to see what your heart reveals to you. Are your actions and motives pure and undefiled before My Father? Ask for My help to keep your heart pure and unspotted from the world in which you live. Always be aware of the evil forces that try to draw you into living a self-centered life.

> For am I now seeking the favor of people, or of God? Or am I striving to please people? If I were still trying to please people, I would not be a bond-servant of Christ.
>
> Galatians 1:10

> For they loved the approval of people rather than the approval of God.
>
> John 12:43

MOVING YOUR MOUNTAINS

───◆───

Your prayers and your praises are rising up before My presence. I am seated on the throne of your heart. The sincerity of your heart causes Me to move your mountains, and toss them into the sea. Have faith to believe that all things are possible when you bow your heart and knee to worship Me. A beautiful aroma arises before Me when you enter into worship and praise. Therefore, continue to offer your sacrifice of praise which is fully pleasing to Me. Give Me thanks for moving your mountains.

> Truly I say to you, whoever says to this mountain, 'Be taken up and thrown into the sea,' and does not doubt in his heart, but believes that what he says is going to happen, it will be *granted* to him.
>
> Mark 11:23

> May my prayer be counted as incense before You; the raising of my hands as the evening offering.
>
> Psalms 141:2

MY DIVINE LIGHT

———•———

My divine light allows you to see the truth illuminated around you. Step into My divine light so you can see the direction that you need to go. Blessings will abound when you stay within the circumference of My light. Walk in the illuminated path lighted for you. Peace and comfort will be a benefit of walking this lighted path. You will not stumble when you can clearly see the path in front of you. Enjoy the blessings that come when you stay in the shadow of My light. Continue walking on the lighted path to enjoy My blessings that will be seen flowing toward you.

> Then Jesus again spoke to them, saying, "I am the Light of the world; the one who follows Me will not walk in the darkness, but will have the Light of life."
>
> John 8:12

> Your word is a lamp to my feet and a light to my path.
>
> Psalms 119:105

MY EYES SEE ALL

———◆———

Even before there is a word on your tongue, I, the Creator of all things, know it all. All of your thoughts are evident to Me before you speak a word. I created your innermost parts, and wove you in your mother's womb. My eyes have seen your formless substance. In My book were written all the days that were ordained for you, when as yet there was not one of them. You are precious in My sight, and My love is greater than anyone can ever know. I pray you receive the gift of My love that was poured out for you.

> For you created my innermost parts; You wove me in my mother's womb.
>
> Psalms 139:13

> Your eyes have seen my formless substance; and in Your book were written all the days that were ordained *for me*, when as yet there was not one of them.
>
> Psalms 139:16

MY FATHER'S GLORY

———◆———

The glory of My Father shines brightly through those who stay close to Me. They reflect My light as they are being transformed by My Holy Spirit. This light reveals truth to those it shines upon. Nothing will be hidden or secret for it will come to light. My love will be manifested to those around you. The power of My love will be bright as the noonday sun. Its warmth will give you the energy to pass it along to others. Let the reflection of My Father's glory shine brightly through you, as you stay ever close to Me.

> *Take care that* no one deceives himself. If anyone among you thinks that he is wise in this age, he must become foolish, so that he may become wise.
>
> I Corinthians 3:18

> By this the love of God was revealed in us, that God has sent His only Son into the world so that we may live through Him.
>
> I John 4:9

MY GIFTS AND CALLING

My gifts and calling to you are not able to be changed. They are irrevocable. Accept these gifts and use them to glorify your Father in heaven. If you are not sure about what these gifts I have given you are, ask and it shall be revealed to you. Stir up these gifts and calling within you, so the plan for your life will be fulfilled. Use your gifts effectively for God's glory. Every person is given gifts and a calling for growth and encouragement to those around you. I will give you the power to use your calling and gifts effectively for the glory of God.

> For the gifts and calling of God are irrevocable.
>
> Romans 11:29

> For this reason I remind you to kindle afresh the gift of God which is in you through the laying on of my hands.
>
> II Timothy 1:6

MY GOOD PLANS

---·❖·---

You cannot be transformed into the person who serves Me wholeheartedly until you have a renewing of your mind. The battle to let go of control of your life is in the mind. Satan uses discouraging thoughts to keep you from moving forward with My plan. My plan is to prosper you and give you a hope and a future. Release your will and control of your life to Me, so that I may give you blessings unspeakable. You are precious in My sight and the apple of My eye. Nothing will be able to separate you from My love. My love is everlasting and unchanging. Embrace My love and move forward with My good plans I have awaiting you.

> And do not be conformed to this world, but be transformed by the renewing of your mind, so that you may prove what the will of God is, that which is good and acceptable and perfect.
>
> Romans 12:2

> For the LORD of armies says this: "After glory He has sent me against the nations that plunder you, for the one who touches you, touches the apple of His eye.
>
> Zechariah 2:8

MY LOVE AND LIGHT

———◆———

The power of My love and light works in and through you to accomplish My will. Your speech can be a powerful demonstration of the Holy Spirit working in and through you. Always remember this power is not from human wisdom, but from the Holy Spirit. Do you know that your body is the temple of the Holy Spirit, who is in you? For you were bought at a price, therefore glorify God in your body and in your spirit which are God's. Show My love wherever you go that My light will shine brightly for all to see. In doing so, you will accomplish My will.

> And my message and my preaching were not in persuasive words of wisdom, but in demonstration of the Spirit and of power.
>
> I Corinthians 2:4
>
> For you have been bought for a price: therefore glorify God in your body.
>
> I Corinthians 6:20

MY PROMISES ARE TRUE

I am the ultimate promise keeper. You can trust that My promises are true, and that I will keep My promises given to you in My Word. You can have total confidence that what I say, I will do. I do not waiver in My love for you. My steadfast love for you endures forever. It is hard for you to comprehend forever, but one day with Me is as a thousand years. Time is like a passing shadow. Be aware of what you use your precious time for.

> Man is like the breath; his days are like a passing shadow.
>
> Psalms 144:4

> For a thousand years in Your sight are like yesterday when it passes by, or *like* a watch in the night.
>
> Psalms 90:4

MY WORD

My Word is like a seed planted within the heart of man. A seed sprouts and grows in good soil. My Word goes forth and flourishes in the heart of man who is ready to receive it. My words have life and grow when nurtured. The seeds grow and produce an abundant harvest, as My Word, also produces an abundant harvest. My Word shall prosper and accomplish what I please. Saturate your heart and mind in the Word of God, that you may have an abundant harvest that glorifies Me. My Word stands forever.

> So will My word be which goes out of My mouth; it will not return to Me empty, without accomplishing what I desire, and without succeeding *in the purpose* for which I sent it.
>
> Isaiah 55:11

> The grass withers, the flower fades, but the word of our God stands forever.
>
> Isaiah 40:8

NOT BY YOUR WORKS

I have saved you and called you with a holy calling, not according to your works, but according to My own purpose and grace. Salvation was My Father's plan, and you can do nothing to earn it by your works. I have completed the work and abolished death by suffering the sins of mankind on the cross. When the perishable will have put on the imperishable, and this mortal will have put on immortality, then will come about the saying that is written, death is swallowed up in victory. Continue living out My purpose and plan for you. Be steadfast and immovable always abounding in doing My work, knowing your toil is not in vain.

> Who saved us and called us with a holy calling, not according to our works, but according to His own purpose and grace, which was granted to us in Christ Jesus from all eternity.
>
> II Timothy 1:9

> But when this perishable puts on the imperishable, and this mortal puts on immortality, then will come about the saying that is written: "Death has been swallowed up in victory."
>
> I Corinthians 15:54

NOTHING IS HIDDEN

———◆———

What is in a man's heart will be revealed, as in the water, face reflects the face. One's true self will be revealed to others and not hidden. For nothing is secret that will not be revealed, nor anything hidden that will not be known and come to light. Choose to live a life with a heart that reflects My love for all people. Hear My words and hold them fast within an honest and good heart. My words will go out from you and not return to Me empty, but will accomplish what I desire. They will also achieve My purpose and prosper everywhere I send them. Remember to carry My words close to your heart and be ready to share them when the occasions arise.

> As in water the face *reflects* the face, so the heart of a person *reflects the* person.
>
> Proverbs 27:19

> For nothing is concealed that will not become evident. Nor *anything* hidden that will not be known and come to light.
>
> Luke 8:17

NURTURE YOUR RELATIONSHIP

———◆———

Make My relationship with you a priority in your life. You cannot grow in your relationship with Me if other people and things are foremost in your thoughts. Where do I fit into your life? Those who take most of your time and attention are a priority. Nurture your relationship with Me. I am a friend who sticks closer than a brother. The more time you spend with Me, the closer our bond will be. This will be pleasing to Me, and help you to be fruitful in your life, and increase in the knowledge of God. Stay in My Word, and grow in your relationship with Me.

> A person of *too many* friends *comes* to ruin, but there is a friend who sticks *closer* than a brother.
>
> Proverbs 18:24

> In the beginning was the Word, and the Word was with God, and the Word was God.
>
> John 1:1

OBEDIENCE BRINGS BLESSINGS

If you follow My leading for your life, and live uprightly, no good thing will I withhold from you. My blessings come to those who live in a manner that is pleasing to Me. Obedience always brings blessings into your life. You will be blessed when you trust in Me and listen for My voice to guide your life. My sheep hear Me when I speak, and they follow My instruction. Their hearts long to please Me, and I long to pour out my blessings on them. Follow Me and receive My blessings.

> For the LORD God is a sun and shield; the LORD gives grace and glory; He withholds no good thing from those who walk with integrity.
>
> Psalms 84:11

> My sheep listen to My voice, and I know them, and they follow Me.
>
> John 10:27

OBSTACLES IN YOUR PATH

I am the one who goes before you and will not lead you astray. I see the path that lays before you, the rocks and terrain that try to block your way. I will help you get over and around the obstacles that lay before you. With Me by your side, nothing will be too difficult to accomplish. I will clear the obstacles from your path and shine My light so you can see how to navigate this terrain. Continue to trust Me to guide you. I will not lead you astray or abandon you. You have nothing to fear with Me by your side.

> And the Lord is the one who is going ahead of you; He will be with you. He will not desert you or abandon you. Do not fear and do not be dismayed."
>
> Deuteronomy 31:8

> And those who know Your name will put their trust in You, for You, Lord, have not abandoned those who seek You.
>
> Psalms 9:10

OMNIPOTENT GOD

Why wouldn't you trust the One Who said, "Yet once more I will shake not only the earth, but also the heaven"? You can trust the omnipotent God, who is not subjected to physical limitations like man is. My Father is all-powerful and in control of all of His creation. He is all-powerful, all-knowing, and present everywhere. We work in unison together, Father, Son, and Holy Spirit. My children feel a connection to one another. They feel a oneness with Us and with each other. You are many parts of one body, and we all belong to each other. Our love is the connecting factor for the body to work in unison and accomplish the will of My Father. Beloved, let's love one another, for love is from God, and everyone who loves has been born of God and knows God.

> And His voice shook the earth then, but now He has promised, saying, "YET ONCE MORE I WILL SHAKE NOT ONLY THE EARTH, BUT ALSO THE HEAVEN."
>
> Hebrews 12:26

> For just as we have many parts in one body and all the body's parts do not have the same function, so we, who are many, are one body in Christ, and individually parts of one another.
>
> Romans 12:4-5

ONE TRUE SHEPHERD

There is only one true Shepherd and one flock. My sheep hear My voice and know Me. You experience My blessings when you stay close to Me. When you start wandering away from Me, I take my staff and lead you back toward Me. When you stay close by your Shepherd, you will experience My protection, guidance, and peace. I am the Good Shepherd who gave His life for the sheep. Remember to stay close to Me to receive My blessings, for I am the one true Shepherd, and the doorway for the sheep.

> "I am the good shepherd; the good shepherd lays down His life for the sheep.
>
> John 10:11

> So Jesus said to them again, "Truly, truly I say to you, I am the door of the sheep."
>
> John 10:7

PATIENCE THROUGH TRIALS

When you go through trials, know that the power of My love is transforming you. I am holding you close as you endure times of trial. Let endurance have its perfect result, so that you may be perfect and complete, lacking in nothing. You will draw closer to Me when you trust Me to help you through these trials. You will see how the stretching of your faith produces patience in you. Growth comes when you go through trials in your life. Remember that this light momentary affliction is preparing you for an eternal weight of glory beyond all comparison.

> And let endurance have *its* perfect result, so that you may be perfect and complete, lacking in nothing.
>
> James 1:4

> For our momentary, light affliction is producing for us an eternal weight of glory far beyond all comparison.
>
> II Corinthians 4:17

PEACE IS A BEAUTIFUL GIFT

When you keep your focus on Me throughout the day, you will have perfect peace. Peace in your heart and mind is such a beautiful gift. Peace is the opposite of anxiety. Peace is a calmness and tranquility of the mind. It is a quiet and restful spirit. When you put your complete trust in Me, you will have the gift of peace. When you call to Me, I will listen to you. If possible, so far as it depends on you, be at peace with all people. Do not be overcome by evil, but overcome evil with good. Trust Me to give you the power to do this.

> The steadfast of mind You will keep in perfect peace, because he trusts in You.
>
> Isaiah 26:3
>
> If possible, so far as it depends on you, be at peace with all people.
>
> Romans 12:18

PLEASE ME

Others who see your external obedience think you are living a righteous life, but I see into your heart. Be a servant who loves and serves Me with your whole heart. Your concern should not be to please man, but to please Me who sees every one of your motives. When your motive is to please man, you are not My servant. Do nothing from selfishness or empty conceit, but with humility of mind regard one another as more important than yourselves. Whatever you do, do your work wholeheartedly, as for the Lord, rather than for men. You know that from the Lord you will receive the reward of the inheritance. It is I, the Lord, whom you serve.

> Do nothing from selfishness or empty conceit, but with humility consider one another as more important than yourselves.
>
> Philippians 2:3

> Whatever you do, do your work heartily, as for the Lord not for people, knowing that *it is* from the Lord *that* you will receive the reward of the inheritance. *It is* the Lord Christ *whom* you serve.
>
> Colossians 3:23-24

PRAYER

---◆---

Prayer is simply talking to Me, having a conversation with a friend. I enjoy listening to your voice and to your thoughts. Share your innermost thoughts with Me. Let Me help you make decisions that will bring joy into your life. When disturbing thoughts come into your mind, rebuke the evil one who tries to discourage you. Use My name to rebuke him and he will flee. Continue in your conversations with Me, and I will help you walk down the path that brings peace and joy into your life.

> You know when I sit down and when I get up; You understand my thought from far away.
>
> Psalms 139:2

> In all your ways acknowledge Him, and He will make your paths straight.
>
> Proverbs 3:6

PRIDE VERSUS HUMILITY

Do not act in a prideful manner, or try and exalt yourself before men. These actions are displeasing to Me. People will turn away from and avoid someone who exalts himself. On the other hand, a person who is humble has a sweet spirit that others want to spend time with. When you humble yourselves before Me, I will exalt you in the proper time. I will resist the proud but give grace to those who are humble. Those who are humble have wisdom and obtained favor from Me. Stay close to Me and question your heart's motives when they seem prideful.

> Therefore humble yourselves under the mighty hand of God, so that He may exalt you at the proper time.
>
> I Peter 5:6

> When pride comes, then comes dishonor; but with the humble there is wisdom.
>
> Proverbs 11:2

REFLECT MY LOVE

———◆———

Are you reflecting My love to others in your daily walk with Me? As you walk along this path of life, is My loving presence visible to those around you? As in water face reflects face so the heart of man reflects the man. When you love one another, all people will know that you are My disciples. I will lead you in the paths of righteousness for My namesake. Be imitators of God as dear children and walk in My love. I have loved you and given Myself for you, as an offering and a sacrifice to My Father, for a sweet-smelling aroma.

> As in water a face *reflects* the face, so the heart of a person *reflects the* person.
> Proverbs 27:19

> Therefore be imitators of God, as beloved children; and walk in love, just as Christ also loved you and gave Himself up for us, an offering and a sacrifice to God as a fragrant aroma.
> Ephesians 5:1-2

RELY ON MY STRENGTH

My life can be demonstrated to others through those who have put their trust in Me. My power can show forth from you even as you go through trials. Rely on Me to sustain and guide you with My strength. You will be able to overcome and have peace from Me, which is a precious gift. Challenges in life will come, but I am there with you and My Spirit lives in you. You are never alone. My Spirit is a guarantee that I will complete the work I have begun in you. For My people walk by faith, not by sight. Trust that My strength will see you through.

> Now He who prepared us for this very *purpose is* God, who gave us the Spirit as a pledge.
>
> 2 Corinthians 5:5

> For we walk by faith, not by sight.
>
> 2 Corinthians 5:7

RENEWED IN YOUR SPIRIT

———◆———

Even though the outward man is perishing, you are being renewed in your spirit every day. The inner you is getting more vibrant and alive in Me. You are growing in a love that penetrates those around you. There is such a drawing to your renewed spirit. It washes over those around you showing My light and love that cannot be explained. There is such a mystery to this precious love light glowing through you to others. It is unexplainable, but very much present in you. This renewal of your spirit is eternal.

> Therefore we do not lose heart, but though our outer person is decaying, yet our inner *person* is being renewed day by day.
>
> II Corinthians 4:16

> And the city has no need of the sun or of the moon to shine on it, for the glory of God has illuminated it, and its lamp *is* the Lamb.
>
> Revelation 21:23

RIVERS OF LIVING WATER

There is an overflowing of the Holy Spirit given to those who accept Me as Lord and Savior. When you accept Me, out of your heart will flow rivers of living water. The wellspring of wisdom is a flowing brook. This wisdom flows like rivers of water from those who are led by My Spirit. Guard your heart from any evil thoughts. Continue to search for the wisdom from above. Commit to serving Me, and your thoughts will be established. I will guard your heart and your mind.

> The one who believes in Me, as the Scripture said, "From his innermost being will flow rivers of living water."
>
> John 7:38

> And the peace of God, which surpasses all comprehension, will guard your hearts and minds in Christ Jesus.
>
> Philippians 4:7

RULER OVER MANKIND

———◆———

Know that My Father, the most high God, is ruler over the realm of mankind. He sets over it whomever He wishes. He gives wisdom to wise men and knowledge to people of understanding. It is He who reveals the profound and hidden things. He knows what is in the darkness, and the light dwells with Him. I am the One who is going ahead of you and will be with you. I will not desert or abandon you. Do not be afraid or upset, for I am watching over you and guiding you along the path of life. I shall be to you an everlasting light, that will shine brightly when your path seems dim.

> It is He who reveals the profound and hidden things; He knows what is in the darkness, and the light dwells with Him.
>
> Daniel 2:22

> And the Lord is the one who is going ahead of you; He will be with you. He will not desert you or abandon you. Do not fear and do not be dismayed.
>
> Deuteronomy 31:8

SEALED WITH THE HOLY SPIRIT

---◆---

When you believed in Me, Jesus Christ, you were sealed with the Holy Spirit of promise. You were anointed with this seal to prove that you belong to Me. This gift of the Holy Spirit is able to set you apart from the world. He gives you the ability to show My love to the lost world. He helps you surrender your will for My will. You will receive power when you receive the Holy Spirit. This power will enable you to be My witnesses to all people you are in contact with. The Holy Spirit has the ability to transform you into an effective witness for Me. The Holy Spirit works in each person for the good of all.

> In Him, you also, after listening to the message of truth, the gospel of your salvation—having also believed, you were sealed in Him with the Holy Spirit of the promise.
>
> Ephesians 1:13

> But to each one is given the manifestation of the Spirit for the common good.
>
> I Corinthians 12:7

SEARCH FOR WISDOM

———◆———

If you seek wisdom as silver and search for wisdom as hidden treasure, you will understand the fear of Me, the Lord. You will find the knowledge of My Father in heaven. From My mouth comes knowledge and understanding. Listen intently for my instruction and move forward with the understanding that you are not alone in performing this task. Try in every circumstance to overcome evil with good. For my thoughts are not your thoughts and My ways are higher than your ways. Continue seeking Me for direction and you will be wise. Cling to Me, and you will receive the peace that surpasses all understanding.

> Do not be overcome by evil, but overcome evil with good.
>
> Romans 12:21

> "For My thoughts are not your thoughts, nor are your ways My ways," declares the Lord.
>
> Isaiah 55:8

SEARCHING FOR HAPPINESS

Are you searching for things to make you happy? Be willing to give of yourselves to others and you will find what you are looking for. All the labor of man is for his mouth, yet the soul is not satisfied. One who loves money will not be satisfied with money, nor one who loves abundance with its income. This too is futility. Sharing with others and giving of your time will bring you joy that satisfies your heart, soul, and mind. Fervently love one another from the heart. By this all people will know that you are My disciples if you have love for one another.

> One who loves money will not be satisfied with money, nor one who loves abundance *with its* income. This too is futility.
>
> Ecclesiastes 5:10

> By this all *people* will know that you are My disciples: if you have love for one another.
>
> John 13:35

SEE AND HEAR TRUTH

———◆———

I bless My children to be able to see with their eyes and to hear with their ears: truth. You will hear My words and understand them. You will be able to bear fruit for the Kingdom when your heart is open to Me. The Holy Spirit will guide you into all truth and tell you things to come. I will be glorified through the work accomplished by the Holy Spirit's leading in your life. The Holy Spirit does not speak on his own authority, but whatever He hears He will speak and declare to you. I will reveal My plan to you when you seek it.

> But blessed are your eyes, because they see; and your ears, because they hear.
>
> Matthew 13:16

> But when He, the Spirit of truth, comes, He will guide you into all the truth; for He will not speak on His own, but whatever He hears, He will speak; and He will disclose to you what is to come.
>
> John 16:13

SERVE ME WITH YOUR WHOLE HEART

My desire would be that you serve Me with your whole heart, not halfheartedly as some do. Much more can be accomplished when I am a priority in your life. Don't allow Me to be an afterthought. Our relationship cannot grow without a determined effort to spend time with Me. You will seek Me and find Me when you seek Me with all your heart. You will be blessed when you keep My statutes and follow My ways. Together we can accomplish many impossible tasks, for with God all things are possible. Make it a priority to seek Me with your whole heart and enjoy a blessed life.

> And you will seek Me and find *Me* when you search for Me with all your heart.
>
> Jeremiah 29:13

> Blessed are those who comply with His testimonies, *and* seek Him with all *their* heart. They also do no injustice; they walk in His ways.
>
> Psalms 119:2-3

SHEDDING OF MY BLOOD

Without the shedding of My blood, there would be no remission of your sins. Complete forgiveness of your sins was accomplished by the shedding of My blood. I have paid the penalty for your sin. There is no greater love than this, that a man lay down his life for his friends. The power of My love is given to those who desire to follow after Me. These things I command you, that you love one another. As My Father has loved Me, so I have loved you. Remain in My love and keep My commandments, for this will show you are abiding in Me.

> This I command you, that you love one another.
>
> John 15:17

> Just as the Father has loved Me, I also have loved you; remain in My love.
>
> John 15:9

SING SONGS OF PRAISE

You give Me joy when you make melody in your heart to Me. When you sing songs of praise and worship to Me, it gives Me blessings to the full. I see your inexpressible and glorious joy as you worship Me through song. Even though you have not seen Me, you show your love for Me through your heartfelt worship. This love is possible in such a powerful way, because of the Holy Spirit who lives within you. Continue expressing your love through songs to Me, Jesus, the lover of your soul.

> Speaking to one another in psalms and hymns and spiritual songs, singing and making melody with your hearts to the Lord.
>
> Ephesians 5:19

> And though you have not seen Him, you love Him, and though you do not see Him now, but believe in Him, you greatly rejoice with joy inexpressible and full of glory.
>
> I Peter 1:8

SPEAK TRUTH

---◆---

I am faithful, speaking truth to all generations. There is not a word on your tongue that I do not know altogether. Nothing is hidden from Me. I detest lying lips, but delight in people who are trustworthy. My children, let us not love with words or speech, but with actions and in truth. Be diligent to present yourself approved to God; a worker who does not need to be ashamed of rightly dividing the Word of truth. Search My Word for it is all truth. My Word will provide you with the map of how to live out truth in your life. It is an instruction to navigate the decisions you must make in your life.

> Lying lips are an abomination to the LORD, but those who deal faithfully are His delight.
>
> Proverbs 12:22

> Be diligent to present yourself approved to God as a worker who does not need to be ashamed, accurately handling the word of truth.
>
> II Timothy 2:15

STAY CLOSELY CONNECTED TO ME

Your fruit of the Spirit will be evident when you stay closely connected to Me. You will flourish when you are getting the proper nutrition from the vine. As the branch cannot bear fruit of itself unless it abides in the vine. As in the natural world, a vine without proper food or water will start to wither. Oh, how much more do you need to stay closely connected to Me to bear fruit for the kingdom? Do not let long lapses of spending time with Me become your normal way of living. When this happens, the branch starts to wither. This is not a healthy way to live your life. For My children to bear much fruit, they must delight in My Word, and meditate on it day and night. They will be like a tree firmly planted by streams of water, which yields fruit in due season. Its leaf does not wither and in whatever they do, they prosper.

> Remain in Me, and I in you. Just as the branch cannot bear fruit of itself but must remain in the vine, so neither *can* you unless you remain in Me.
>
> John 15:4

> He will be like a tree planted by streams of water, which yields its fruit in its season, and its leaf does not wither; and in whatever he does, he prospers.
>
> Psalms 1:3

STAY PLUGGED INTO ME

———◆———

When you stay plugged into Me your light will be bright. Those around you will be able to see Me in you. The light has a warmth and drawing power. You enjoy basking in the bright sunlight. I am the light of the world. The one who follows Me will not walk in darkness, but will have the light of life. When I am the light of your life, you are made alive together with Me. For by grace you have been saved through faith, and this is not of yourselves, it is the gift of God. No greater gift can anyone receive in life. Remember to stay plugged into Me so your light will be bright.

> Then Jesus again spoke to them, saying, "I am the Light of the world; the one who follows Me will not walk in the darkness, but will have the Light of life."
>
> John 8:12

> For by grace you have been saved through faith; and this *is* not of yourselves, *it is* the gift of God.
>
> Ephesians 2:8

STEP INTO MY THOUGHT PATTERN

I will comfort you in the multitude of your anxieties. Turn your thoughts back to Me when you become anxious about what is going on around you. Step into my thought pattern to lift you above your circumstances. I hold the key that unlocks the power to strengthen you in all wisdom and spiritual understanding. This will help you be fruitful in every good work and increase your knowledge in My Father who sent Me. Set your mind on things above where I am seated at the right hand of my Father.

> When my anxious thoughts multiply within me, Your comfort delights my soul.
>
> Psalms 94:19

> So that you will walk in a manner worthy of the Lord, to please *Him* in all respects, bearing fruit in every good work and increasing in the knowledge of God.
>
> Colossians 1:10

SURRENDER YOUR WILL

Surrender your will to Me so you can be fully used for the furtherance of the Kingdom of God. Do not be conformed to this world, but be transformed by the renewing of your mind, that you may prove what is that good and acceptable and perfect will of God. Start your day by surrendering it to Me. Focus your thoughts on Me and the plan I have for you. I give you the strength to accomplish the task I lay before you. I am the one who goes with you and will not fail you or forsake you. I will keep you in perfect peace when your mind is stayed on Me because you trust in Me.

> The one who has found his life will lose it, and the one who has lost his life on My account will find it.
> Matthew 10:39

> Have I not commanded you? Be strong and courageous! Do not be terrified nor dismayed, for the Lord your God is with you wherever you go.
> Joshua 1:9

TAKE EVERY THOUGHT CAPTIVE

When chaos and turmoil are all around you, know that We created the heavens and the earth. I am listening to your prayers and working behind the scenes to move you to a place of peace and tranquility in your heart and mind. Guard your thoughts, for the battle is in your mind. Take every thought captive to obeying Me. Know that thoughts of fear and doubt are not from Me. Rebuke Satan's attack of your mind and turn your thoughts back to trusting Me. For you wrestle not against flesh and blood, but against principalities, powers, and the rulers of the darkness of this world.

> This is the confidence which we have before Him, that, if we ask anything according to His will, He hears us.
>
> I John 5:14

> For our struggle is not against flesh and blood, but against the rulers, against the powers, against the world forces of this darkness, against the spiritual *forces* of wickedness in the heavenly *places.*
>
> Ephesians 6:12

TALENTS GIVEN

———◆———

Talents given are to be used and not hidden. Don't miss opportunities given to use your talents to further the kingdom of My Father in heaven. You show yourself faithful when you use your given talents wisely. When you step out in faith believing and trusting, then I will show you multiple ways to use these talents. Each of you should use whatever gift or talent you have received to serve others as faithful stewards of the grace of God. My Father will give you the strength to accomplish the task He has given you to do. My Father gives strength to the weary, and to the one who lacks might He increases power. Use your talents wisely.

> As each one has received a *special* gift, employ it in serving one another as good stewards of the multifaceted grace of God.
>
> I Peter 4:10

> He gives strength to the weary, and to *the one who* lacks might He increases power.
>
> Isaiah 40:29

THE BEAUTY OF MY WORD

Let the beauty of My Word permeate your heart and lift your soul to the heavens. Let peace flow over you like a wave of the sea, that removes all the stressors from your mind. Embrace the calming peace of My presence lifting you to higher ground. Hold fast to your faith without wavering. Choose to rest in the center of My will, keeping My words ever flowing in your heart and mind. Let My words become a joy to you and the delight of your heart. Partake of My Word daily and savor it in your heart.

> In peace I will both lie down and sleep, for You alone, Lord, have me dwell in safety.
>
> Psalms 4:8

> Let the word of Christ richly dwell within you, with all wisdom teaching and admonishing one another with psalms, hymns, *and* spiritual songs, singing with thankfulness in your hearts to God.
>
> Colossians 3:16

THE BREAD OF LIFE

———◆———

The eating of physical food, such as bread, gives nutrients for sustaining life in the body. When you pray, "Give us this day our daily bread," you are asking for your needs to be met. I am faithful to meet your needs. If you believe in Me, you partake in the Bread of life, who came down from heaven. I am the living Bread. When you eat of this bread, you will live forever. This bread is necessary for sustaining everlasting life in you. Pray to receive this sustaining bread of life and enjoy life everlasting.

> I am the bread of life.
>
> John 6:48
>
> This is the bread that comes down out of heaven, so anyone may eat from it and not die.
>
> John 6:50

THE INSTRUCTION MANUAL

My Word is an instruction manual on how to live a fulfilled life. Pray for Me to open your understanding that you might comprehend what I am teaching you in My Word. Reading My Word daily will give you principles to live by. Its guidance will impart wisdom on how to respond to difficult situations in your life. My Word is alive and active, sharper than any two-edged sword. It penetrates deep down into your heart and your mind. Keep these precious words foremost in your mind so you may recall them when important decisions need to be made.

> Take hold of instruction; do not let go. Guard her, for she is your life.
>
> Proverbs 4:13

> For the word of God is living and active, and sharper than any two-edged sword, even penetrating as far as the division of soul and spirit, of both joints and marrow, and able to judge the thoughts and intentions of the heart.
>
> Hebrews 4:12

THE POWER OF MY SPIRIT

How you live your life in front of others speaks volumes to a watching world. The world is watching for you to fail. I want you to act in the same manner yesterday, today, and forever. Show My love through My power regardless of your circumstances. You will be able to do exceedingly abundantly above all that you ask or think according to My power that works in you. I am equipping you for the work of the ministry, and for the uplifting of those who follow Me. Let us consider how to stir up and encourage one another to love and good works. Ask Me daily to help you live a life that shows the power of My Spirit, to a watching world.

> Now to him who is able to do far more abundantly beyond all that we ask or think, according to the power that works within us.
>
> Ephesians 3:20

> And let's consider how to encourage one another in love and good deeds.
>
> Hebrews 10:24

THE POWER OF WORDS

―――◆―――

Consider the power of My words spoken, how I spoke, "Let there be light," and there was light. All creation evolved by the power of My words spoken. God said, "Let us make man in our image, according to our likeness," and it was so. Your mind cannot comprehend this kind of power of spoken words. Words are much more powerful than realized. Think about letting the words of your mouth be acceptable in My sight. Let your speech always be with grace seasoned with salt, so My wisdom will flow from your lips.

> Then God said, "Let there be light"; and there was light.
>
> Genesis 1:3

> May the words of my mouth and the meditation of my heart be acceptable in Your sight, Lord, my rock and my Redeemer.
>
> Psalms 19:14

THE RIGHTEOUSNESS OF GOD

I bore your sins on the cross that you might become the righteousness of God through Me. I had no sin but endured the penalty of crucifixion on the cross for your sins. My crucifixion made it possible to be reconciled back to My Father. Receive this precious gift, and realize that all things have become new. Reach out in love to help others be reconciled back to My Father. In the beginning, it was Our desire to have a close relationship with man. Walk close to Me now and seek My presence. You have been washed clean by My blood, being made righteous by the power of the Holy Spirit who lives in you.

> He made Him who knew no sin *to be* sin in our behalf, so that we might become the righteousness of God in Him.
>
> II Corinthians 5:21

> If Christ is in you, though the body is dead because of sin, yet the spirit is alive because of righteousness.
>
> Romans 8:10

THE ULTIMATE INHERITANCE

———◆———

You are connected to your family through a bloodline. As a family heir, you are entitled to inherit property. When you accept Me as Lord and Savior of your life, you become an heir of God through Me. You become sons and daughters through My blood poured out for you. You are sealed with the Holy Spirit promised, which reveals you belong in My bloodline. You become heirs with God and joint-heirs with Me. This entitles you to inherit the Kingdom of God and have a residence in heaven.

> Therefore you are no longer a slave, but a son; and if a son, then an heir through God.
>
> Galatians 4:7

> And if you belong to Christ, then you are Abraham's descendants, heirs according to promise.
>
> Galatians 3:29

THE WILL OF MY FATHER

———◆———

I came down from heaven to save and to serve mankind. This is the will of My Father who sent Me, that everyone who believes in Me may have everlasting life. I will raise him up at the last day. My mind was focused and centered on fulfilling the will of My Father who sent Me. I prayed to My Father saying, Oh My Father, if it is possible, let this cup pass from Me, yet not as I will, but as You will. All authority has been given to Me in heaven and on earth. My heart's desire is to do the will of My Father. I pray this will also be your desire, to fulfill the will of My Father in your life.

> And this is the will of Him who sent Me, that of everything He has given Me I will lose nothing, but will raise it up on the last day.
>
> John 6:39

> And He went a little beyond *them*, and fell on His face and prayed, saying, "My Father, if it is possible, let this cup pass from Me; yet not as I will, but as You *will*."
>
> Matthew 26:39

THINGS SEEN ARE TEMPORARY

Everything your eyes see in this world are temporary, but the things which are not seen are eternal. You live and walk by faith, not by what you see. I am behind the scenes working on your behalf. Trust Me to guide you along the road of life. I will teach you My way that you may walk in truth along My path. For My ways are right and those who are upright walk in them. For all that is in the world, the lust of the flesh, and the lust of the eyes, and the boastful pride of life, are not from My Father, but from the world. The world is passing away, but the one who does the will of My Father lives forever.

> While we look not at the things which are seen, but at the things which are not seen; for the things which are seen are temporal, but things which are not seen are eternal.
>
> II Corinthians 4:18
>
> The world is passing away and *also* its lusts; but the one who does the will of God continues *to live* forever.
>
> I John 2:17

THINKING PATTERNS

———— ♦ ————

Your thoughts skip around from subject to subject, keeping you from concentrating and thinking clearly. When this starts to happen, bring your focus back on Me. I will help you sort out your thoughts and give you clarity for the path ahead. Always include Me in your decision-making. It will make your life flow more easily. Remember My eyes saw your substance before you were formed. Even before you say a word, I already know it. I am ever around you, ready to assist you when you call out to Me.

> LORD, You have searched me and known *me*.
>
> Psalms 139:1

> Your eyes have seen my formless substance; and in Your book were written all the days that were ordained *for me*, when as yet there was not one of them.
>
> Psalms 139:16

TRADITIONS OF MEN

When you reject My Father's commandments to keep your traditions, I am not first place in your life. This shows Me you want your own way, and do not follow My leading. You are living for your own selfish desires. My desire would be that you love Me with all of your heart, with all of your soul, and with all of your strength. My ways are best, and when I have first place, you will be blessed. You worship Me in vain when your main desire is to keep man's traditions. Ask Me to create a clean heart in you and renew a right spirit within you.

> He was always saying to them, "You are experts at setting aside the commandment of God in order to keep your tradition."
>
> Mark 7:9

> And you shall love the LORD your God with all your heart and with all your soul and with all your strength.
>
> Deuteronomy 6:5

TRANSGRESSIONS REMOVED

———◆———

I have removed your transgressions as far as the East is from the West, to remember them no more. You need to remove them from your mind, and not allow the evil one to continue bringing them up. Just rebuke him, in My name, and he will have to flee. Let us move forward with a clean slate. Begin your day with Me praying and reading in My Word to give you the protection and positive flow for the day. Join Me in My plan to give you fulfillment for your life. A satisfaction in a life well-lived, where contentment and peace reign. Choose to move forward with Me guiding you down the path of life everlasting.

> As far as the east is from the west, so far has He removed our wrongdoings from us.
>
> Psalms 103:12

> Submit therefore to God. But resist the devil, and he will flee from you.
>
> James 4:7

TREASURES IN MY WORD

―――◆―――

You are standing in My shadow of protection. There is safety when you abide in My presence. Practice keeping your mind centered on Me, and you will feel My presence engulfing your being. My spirit lives in you teaching you all truth. The light of My love inspires you to reach out and touch the world with My love. Fill your heart with the treasures found in My Word. It will inspire you to live a life worthy of My Father, who calls you and is pleased to give you the Kingdom. Let My Spirit continue to fill your cup as you open My Word and digest it.

> One who dwells in the shelter of the Most High will lodge in the shadow of the Almighty.
>
> Psalms 91:1

> Do not be afraid, little flock, because your Father has chosen to give you the kingdom.
>
> Luke 12:32

TROUBLED THOUGHTS

———◆———

Breathe in the breath of My presence. Release any unwanted thoughts that are troubling you. Focus now on My presence lifting you up above your circumstances. I will enable you to soar above the concerns that you may encounter today. Remember that I am ever-present with you, holding your hand. Trust that I will never leave you alone. There is perfect peace in My presence. Stop and remember to breathe in my presence. It will give you the power to overcome any trouble you encounter today.

> The Spirit of God has made me, and the breath of the Almighty gives me life.
>
> Job 33:4

> The steadfast of mind You will keep in perfect peace, because he trusts in You.
>
> Isaiah 26:3

TRUE WISDOM

———•———

The wisdom of this world is foolishness with My Father in heaven. Do not glory in man who claims to be all-wise, for he is a fool. Do not boast about man and what he can do. My Father, who sent Me, is all-wise. He has chosen the foolish things of the world to put to shame the wise. You would be wise to trust in Me and the provision of Salvation offered to all who accept Me as Lord. True wisdom is more precious than gold. Exercise wisdom in your life by trusting Me to guide you throughout your days.

> For the wisdom of this world is foolishness in the sight of God. For it is written: "*He is* THE ONE WHO CATCHES THE WISE BY THEIR CRAFTINESS."
>
> I Corinthians 3:19

> But God has chosen the foolish things of the world to shame the wise, and God has chosen the weak things of the world to shame the things which are strong,
>
> I Corinthians 1:27

UNLOCK TRUE JOY

True happiness will be a benefit to those who lose their life for My sake. In essence, you will have the abundant life by seeking Me to guide your life. If you choose to keep control of your life, you will lose out on the happy abundant life. I hold the key to unlocking true joy and happiness in your life. I desire for you to have this happy, and joy-filled life. When you give Me your will, the door will be open for you to receive the abundant life. For whoever desires to save his life, will lose it, but whoever loses his life for My sake will find it.

> For whoever wants to save his life will lose it; but whoever loses his life for My sake will find it.
>
> Matthew 16:25

> You will make known to me the way of life; in Your presence is fullness of joy; in Your right hand there are pleasures forever.
>
> Psalms 16:11

WAIT ON ME

When you wait on Me for My timing in answering your prayers, you will have victory over the enemy. Remember that I see the beginning and the ending of the situation. Do not be anxious about whether I have heard your request, for I am in the process of getting you results. There are times when I say no to a request because it is not in alignment with My will for you. Accept that I know what is the very best for your life. Delight yourself in Me, and I will give you the desires of your heart.

> Wait for the Lord; be strong and let your heart take courage; yes, wait for the Lord.
>
> Psalms 27:14

> Delight yourself in the Lord; and He will give you the desires of your heart.
>
> Psalms 37:4

WALK UPRIGHTLY

———◆———

No good thing will I withhold from those who walk uprightly. Living your life in service to Me will bring untold blessings into your life. It honors Me when you walk uprightly with integrity. I protect you when you take refuge in Me. I am a shield to those who put their trust in Me. I am a stronghold when trouble comes, and I know those who take refuge in Me. Give careful thought to the path that you walk and be steadfast in all your ways. Live a life of integrity that pleases Me. Reject temptation and walk in an upright manner.

> For the LORD God is a sun and shield; the LORD gives grace and glory; He withholds no good thing from those who walk with integrity.
>
> Psalms 84:11
>
> Every word of God is pure; He is a shield to those who take refuge in Him.
>
> Proverbs 30:5

WE ARE ONE

When you talk with Me, you talk with My Father who sent Me. I and My Father are one. The Father is in Me and I in Him. We desire this oneness with you, as the Holy Spirit lives in you connecting us all. This Holy Spirit testifies with your spirit that you are God's children. You are adopted into the family of God by the Spirit of God. You have the assurance that nothing can separate us from My Father's love. These words are truth coming down from your Father in heaven. Embrace these words and keep them close in your heart and mind.

> I and the Father are one.
>
> John 10:30

> The Spirit Himself testifies with our spirit that we are children of God.
>
> Romans 8:16

WISDOM AND UNDERSTANDING

―――♦―――

Wisdom and understanding are more precious to attain than silver and gold. You will have My blessings when you seek wisdom and understanding. He who loves silver will not be satisfied with silver or he who loves abundance with increase. This is all vanity. No true satisfaction comes from looking at acquired wealth. Happy is the one who finds wisdom and gains understanding. These essential gifts will allow you to have sweet slumber. All the things you may desire cannot compare to having wisdom and understanding. Be wise and seek these spiritual gifts.

> How much better it is to get wisdom than gold! And to get understanding is to be chosen above silver.
>
> Proverbs 16:16

> One who loves money will not be satisfied with money, nor one who loves abundance *with its* income. This too is futility.
>
> Ecclesiastes 5:10

WORDS HEAL OR WOUND

Choose the words you speak wisely. Wise men store up knowledge, but with a foolish mouth ruin stands at the door. Words spoken can heal a weary soul or can wound and break a spirit. Be ever so careful of the words you speak, for they cannot be taken back. Watch over your heart with all diligence, for from it flows the springs of life. For what is in your heart will flow out of your mouth. Seek to guard your heart and mind through Me, and I will renew your mind. Seek to let the words of your mouth and the meditation of your heart be acceptable to Me, for I am your strength and your redeemer.

> Wise people store up knowledge, but with the mouth of the foolish, ruin is at hand.
>
> Proverbs 10:14

> Watch over your heart with all diligence, for from it *flow* the springs of life.
>
> Proverbs 4:23

WORSHIP ME IN SONG

———◆———

You can find joy in Me even in the midst of difficult times in your life. You need to focus your thoughts on Me when trials come. Sing worship music to Me, and the trial will fade into the background. The act of worship will allow you to relax and enjoy My blessing of peace. Get into the habit of starting your day with praise and worship to Me, the rock of your Salvation. Let your voice soar to the heavens and lift your spirit upward. Peace and contentment will be a benefit of your praise and worship to Me.

> Let the word of Christ richly dwell within you, with all wisdom teaching and admonishing one another with psalms, hymns, *and* spiritual songs, singing with thankfulness in your hearts to God.
>
> Colossians 3:16

> Come, let's sing for joy to the LORD, let's shout joyfully to the rock of our salvation.
>
> Psalms 95:1

YOUR FAITH

You show Me your faith when you act in obedience to My direction for you, even when it does not make sense to you. Without faith, it is impossible to please Me. You will be rewarded when you diligently seek Me. You will be satisfied when you follow the path I am leading you down. Embrace the promises I have given you in My Word. The promise that I will fight for you, you only need to be still. The promise that I give strength to the weary and will increase the power of the weak. The promise to give you a peace that transcends all understanding, as well as many more promises in My Word.

> And without faith it is impossible to please *Him*, for the one who comes to God must believe that He exists, and *that* He proves to be One who rewards those who seek Him.
>
> Hebrews 11:6

> Do you not know? Have you not heard? The Everlasting God, the LORD, the Creator of the ends of the earth Does not become weary or tired. His understanding is unsearchable.
>
> Isaiah 40:28

YOUR HAIRS ARE NUMBERED

———◆———

I am concerned about every detail of your life, for the very hairs of your head are all numbered. Do not fear what the future holds, but know I will be with you every step of the way. Keep your mind focused on Me, and what we are doing today. Therefore, do not worry about tomorrow, for tomorrow will worry about its own things. Continue trusting Me for the needs of today, and I will make your paths straight. When you trust Me, I will act on your behalf. My love for you is certain and sure, for I change not.

> But even the hairs of your head are all counted.
>
> Matthew 10:30

> So do not worry about tomorrow; for tomorrow will worry about itself. Each day has enough trouble of its own.
>
> Matthew 6:34

YOUR HEART SPEAKS

———◆———

Thoughts of your heart and mind cannot be hidden, for out of the abundance of the heart the mouth speaks. What is deep within you will come out of you. Even when you try to suppress and hide what is in your heart, it will ultimately be revealed. If your heart is good, then good things will be revealed to others. If your heart is evil, then evil will be revealed for all to see. For by your words spoken you will be justified, or by your words spoken, you will be condemned. It will be known to all what is in your heart by the words you speak.

> You offspring of vipers, how can you, being evil, express *any* good things? For the mouth speaks from that which fills the heart.
>
> Matthew 12:34
>
> For by your words you will be justified, and by your words you will be condemned.
>
> Matthew 12:37

YOUR STEPS ARE ORDERED

―――◆―――

I will give you rest from the days of adversity. Continue trusting Me to guide you along the path of life I have laid out for you. Your steps have been ordered by Me. I will give you favor when you trust Me to guide your days. I will open doors for you to walk through, so that My will can be accomplished through you. Do not fear what lies ahead of you, but hold onto my hand tightly. We will walk this journey of life together.

> The steps of a man are established by the Lord, and He delights in his way.
>
> Psalms 37:23

> Whatever you do, do your work heartily, as for the Lord and not for people.
>
> Colossians 3:23

ABOUT THE AUTHOR

Brenda Sue Randolph was born and raised in the beautiful, majestic mountains of West Virginia. Indiana has been home for thirty-eight years. She has a deep desire to live a life dedicated to serving God. Her first step of obedience proved to her that God would give her all she needed to accomplish the tasks He asked of her. Obedience brought many blessings into her life. Living for God is an adventure that is exciting and so very rewarding.